the human
condition

the human condition

Carmine Gothard

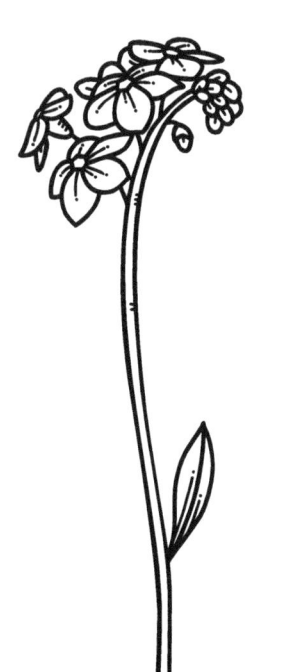

Charleston, SC
www.PalmettoPublishing.com

The Human Condition

Copyright © 2021 by Carmine Gothard

All rights reserved

No portion of this book may be reproduced, stored in a retrieval system, or transmitted in any form by any means—electronic, mechanical, photocopy, recording, or other—except for brief quotations in printed reviews, without prior permission of the author.

First Edition

Paperback ISBN: 978-1-63837-212-7

"Perhaps when we find ourselves wanting everything, it is because we are dangerously close to wanting nothing."

—Sylvia Plath

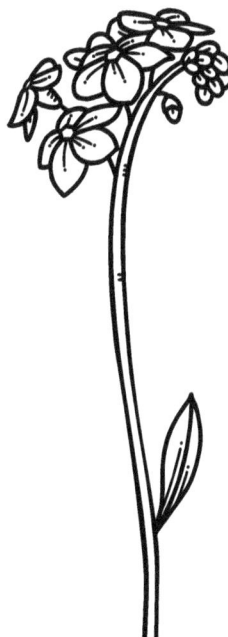

the world did not begin
with a bang
or a whisper

(but simply a gentle warmth)

when they woke in the morning
all that was left was a small light,

fragile, but warm

(how it beat, quietly)

call her hope
call her familiar
call her truth
call her everything

all of the beautiful things in this world
started with wreckage,

at least that's the way the poets like to tell it-
everything worth being
and loving
and believing
came from a place of utter brokenness

("and then there was light"
means nothing without first knowing that there was only
darkness)

I do not mind being alone-
I just don't want to be insignificant

find me softly
for I am still searching
for what it means to be human

Icarus soars through the empty air
and *my god*
this is what it feels like to breathe

bright
and bronze
and unbroken

(but the sun so often burns the ones she loves)

his lungs collapse
as he drowns in the smoke of his own being
and flames spill from his ribcage,
setting fire to the sky

-sunset

speak to me in flowers today

their gentle whispers
will be much easier for me
to understand

tonight I need you to love me

              softly

                      for I am

collapsing under the weight of being

when I said
I would love you
no matter what
I couldn't possibly have known
that no matter what
would mean learning to love
the way you are
without me.

you and me.

that was supposed to be the wonder keeping the stars apart.

but now the constellations are colliding
and I don't know what to do

tonight, is one of those cloudy nights
when you just need the streetlamps
to look like stars

12/28

it was the first time
in a long time
that I was truly scared of losing you

and while
I
know that you are
stronger
than sharp silver and
highway overpasses,
I don't know if
you
know that

"Do you believe in God?" she asked.

I looked down at my hands and tried not to scratch at the barely healed scabs on the back of them. The sounds from the heart rate monitor echoed in my silence.

When I was eight years old I went to my third confession. I always chose to sit in the closed off space where Father couldn't see my face- couldn't see my shame.

As always, the confessions started to pour out of my mouth, as if I couldn't let them go fast enough.

 I hit my brother today. I lied about doing my homework. Yesterday my mom asked me to clean my room and I just shoved everything under my bed. A man touched me and told me to not tell anyone. I convinced my little brother that watermelon seeds would grow watermelons in his stomach. I picked a flower from the neighbors yard and felt so bad I cried, but the flower wouldn't go back to how it was before I ruined it.

Father took a moment to respond before he asked me a few questions about the man, and told me to tell my mom and say three Hail Mary's.

That day I said the prayers, but nothing else.

Twelve years later, I went back for the first time.

"Father forgive me, it has been twelve years, since my last confession, and one year since I last attended Mass."

"I'm starting to fall in love with someone and I don't know what to do. They're with someone else, and I'm trying not to be a bad person."

"Falling in love is not a sin. It is what you choose to do about those feelings that make you the kind of person you are."

"What do I do if I can't stop falling in love with her? I don't want to be a bad person Father."

The priest paused for an uncomfortable moment before addressing me in a different tone all together.

"You are saying you love another girl?"

"Well, yes Father, but-"

"I want you to pray the rosary three times every night and ask God for forgiveness for your sins after each prayer."

"But I thought you said falling in love wasn't a sin."

"Falling in love with a boy isn't a sin. But my child, this type of love is unnatural and unholy. You must pray for forgiveness."

I finally answer her. "I used to. But I'm not so sure these days."

we are by definition
constantly falling short of something breathtaking-
and the weight of every almost
presses down on me
when I try to think of myself as anything more than
something that hadn't quite reached its potential

you tell people "almost carries no weight"
but
on rooftop ledges
and highway overpasses,

it does.

Sunday Mornings

I wonder what the rain would say if she
were able to speak in more than the few
quiet heartbeats of Morse code she leaves to
us on this drizzly Sunday morning. "Me"
and "You" quickly turns into "Us" and "We"
as we curl up by the window's grey/blue
light. "I. Love. You. I Love. You. I. Love. You.
"I. Love. You." she whispers. Can't you hear
her speaking in her gentle thunderstorm?
Kiss me softly while the world is falling
because no one's touch is quite as calming
as yours. Breathe me in until I forget
that before you, I have never known warmth
like this. I'll wish for sunlight... but not yet.

Love Me with the Lights On

I am holding hands with a girl who feels like the first ounce of morning peeking through after the dark. Coffee shops have always been a safe sort of refuge, the smell of chai filters through the air as we talk about love and life and everything in between. Hazy sunlight pours in through the windows, and I am falling in love with the warmth of it all. My fingertips trace over the inside of her wrist. This is the summer of soft lightning and gentle rain, love poems whispered behind the safety of locked bedroom doors, and stolen cigarette butts flicked across the sky like shooting stars. She starts to talk science, and I am suddenly learning about human anatomy in an entirely new way.

Love, teach me about the way two people can breathe into one another, how that will be enough for them to live forever. I want to know where the best place is for me to plant flowers inside of your bones, so you will always have a garden. Show me how it was possible for you to fit the entire ocean in your eyes-

Tell me what it is that makes your heart beat.

I could have listened for hours.

But a man walks in and stops in front of us. His gaze is stuck on our hands, and I grip her tighter.

We leave half-finished coffee and a little bit of ourselves on the table.

I hold her close as we walk past. I am caught breathless between him and the door, and just loud enough for the shop to hear,

"Fucking dykes."

But then we're out in the sun and I can breathe again, and we're safe and I reach for her hand-

and she lets go.

———

I am dating a girl whose eyes hold the seven seas behind them. She parks the car and I am wishing for more of her. Half an hour between work and staff meetings was enough time to drive to start falling, but I am still stuck wading in the shallows.

Darling, I want to dive in deep. I have seen you look up every so often, and I know that those eyes are capable of sinking ships far greater than those I could possibly imagine. I'm not just here for an afternoon swim, give me a flashlight and I will find my way through your darkest parts.

The alarm on my phone goes off before I can say anything. We kiss goodbye in the shelter of the car, again, something so fast.

A quick peck on the lips and half a latte is all I could give to the girl who breathes life into life itself.
I am sprinting through the school to get to the staff meeting, and once I find a seat among my colleagues, time slows to a stop. We need to teach our kids to be kinder and work on making our school a more joyful experience, we're told. We need to encourage them to play nicely with their friends. And also, "Someone broke the clock in the gym." Meeting adjourned.

Except, "Carmine, can you stay a minute?"

Mr. Thomston: "We do not tolerate any form of PDA at this school."
Ms. Wayne: "This is a professional environment."
Mrs. Haux: "This is a warning, the next time we are going to have to let you go."
A chorus of ignorance rises, and with it, a sharpened reminder that my body is taking up far too much innocent space: "There are children here."

But we were also children. Two girls, falling into the oceans of one another, two girls, dancing to fluttering heartbeats in summer storms, two girls and first kisses and new love.

But I am professional. This hasn't made me any less of a good teacher. My kids are so wonderful, and so kind. And I'm the one who broke the clock in the gym, but my kids and I had a hell of a great time with it, learning that not everyone is perfect.

I thought it was safe to give her a quick kiss goodbye in the shelter of our own car.

I am so sorry for loving wrong.

And my god... do I wish my words would have worked.

When I told the girl with oceans for eyes, she secretly sunk every ship on the horizon. A storm built up inside of her, and though the thunder crashed so violently behind closed doors, she never picked me up from work again.

―――

I am kissing a girl who tastes like stardust. I didn't know the stars had a flavor until she brought me in close, and they tasted like ambition and fire with a lingering hope tangled up in the mess. I am holding the other part of me, the essence of why I am who I am. And, for the moment, I am safe.

Let me create new constellations across your collarbones. I want to trace the universe of your spine and breathe in the galaxies you breathe out. Let me climb into your skies, you, my love, are made entirely of star stuff.

She walks me out to my car late at night and leans in through the window. And she wants to kiss me and I want to kiss her, but a woman walks by with her dog, so we give each other a gentle squeeze and leave it at that.

I am running through a field of flowers with her and everything is in full bloom, but it is also broad daylight and I cannot risk it. There are children here. Someone might see, and that might just be the end of it all.

We are entwined on the couch in her basement, the door locked behind us. The girl who tastes like starstuff is running her fingertips up and down the inside of my forearm, and I am counting her ribs like rosary beads.

Forgive me Father for I have sinned, but give me the chance, and I would do it all again.

She gets up and turns off the light before coming back. And we both breathe a little easier.

Some darkness is just safer than others.

―――――

I am in love with a girl who feels like home. She is snowflakes caught on my tongue under streetlamps, smeared lipstick and expensive whiskey, messy hair that smells like vanilla and running and running and running. I am constantly finding her in champagne kisses and dandelion wishes, rose petals on top of satin and lavender buds on white linen, nightlights, and summer storms – she is in every way, every bit of light in this life. I fall asleep to our matching heartbeats, and wake with my ear pressed against her chest, every thump, every drum, every inhale, every beat of her heart, echoes of home, and she is all I have ever wanted love to be.

We are making our way across campus, and her arm wraps itself around my waist. A group of boys walk across the street, eyes fixed on us, and I shrink away.

Darling, love me still, but love me softly.

The boys are next to us and I can't breathe. I am falling to the sidewalk in the chalk outline of a body. Yellow tape wraps itself around my heart and my hands and

Caution: Please step back
Caution: I can only love you in the dark
Caution: Please turn off the lights because that is the only place I feel safe enough to be with you.

Her hand finds a place in mine and she holds me close. "I dare you to take this away from me," she whispers to the wind.

And for the first time, I kiss her, with all of the lights on.

12/17
(Inspired by Phil Kay's "Repetition")

  Love me soft, but love me hard. The love of my life has whiskey on her lips and misadventure in her eyes as she pushes me up against the wall. Her crew team knows, making their parties safe places for us to exist. Everyone's bringing a date has somehow filled the house with forty people or so, but they keep the lights down low and the music up loud. Her lips are warm, we stumble and fall backwards onto a nearby couch, and she's on my lap, and I'm in love- and despite the fact that we are on the edge of a crowded room, I kiss her back like the world is ending.

  And then it does.

  The college football players stand in the corner, embarrassed that they accidentally turned the flash on during their photo shoot. They don't know it was anything more than two drunk girls at a party. They don't know that they captured it all.

Photo series: The End. A Progression.
Two girls, still in love

Two girls, sipping on Bacardi, slipping into a false sense of security
Two girls, think the room is dark enough for them to be together
Two girls falling so far into one another, they aren't quite sure which way is up anymore
Two girls, looking at the camera
Two girls, jumping away from each other
One girl, coming back
One girl, still in love
One of the girls looks like she doesn't quite want to be breathing
The other looks like she doesn't care

Semantic satiation is the psychological phenomenon that occurs when you repeat something over and over again until it loses all meaning.

Gay. Gay. Gay. Gay. Gay. Gay. Gay.

The word or phrase is then perceived as nothing but sound.

Forever. Forever. Forever. Forever. Forever.

See?

"I cannot love you outside of this room" and her heart broke
"I don't want to be out anymore, I can't keep feeling like I'm not a person."

And I was saying sorry like I had never said it before

I look in the mirror, and don't recognize anything.

Carmine.
Carmine Carmine
Carmine Carmine Carmine
Carmine Carmine Carmine Carmine
CarmineCarmineCarmineCarmineCarmineCarmine

And then my fist is forcing its way through my reflection to make sure I am still real.

Sitting amongst shattered fragments on the bedroom floor, I think about how even if I try until the end of forever, I will never be able to put everything back just the way it was, and my heart keeps beating despite my desperate pleas for it to stop.

I love you. I love you. I love you. STOP
I love you. I love you. STOP
I love you. STOP
I love you. I love you. I love you. STOP
I love you. I love you. STOP
I love you. STOP

I love you. (It is so cold without you, and I cannot find the sun)

I love you. (I don't know how to get back home or where home even is anymore)

I love you. (Please. Love me back)

I love you.

See? Nothing.

-For Casey

bare feet on a glass scale-
the beginning of an end

it is so dark and quiet and my heart is beating entirely too fast
I'm scared it's going to stop
it has before-

   twice
(maybe three times)

     (you kind of start to lose track)

stop. START. stop. START.
stop START stop
STOP stop
STOP
STOP
STOP

———

it is so easy to stop being hungry
when your lungs
ache with every breath

you take
this body
starts to shake
and these bones
begin to break
and the heart rate slows.

    and slows.

    and slows.

    build yourself smaller until you disappear-

    smaller

    smaller

    always smaller

    -you can't break something that isn't there

here is a girl: becoming.
carefully calculated collarbones collapsing
under the weight of being

here is a girl: in between.

plant flowers in the hollow spaces inside her bones
so she'll

   grow up

      to be a garden

   grow up

      to be perfect

   grow up

      to be something
   grow up

      to be enough

      they tell her "you can be ANYTHING"

         but what they mean is "you have to be EVERYTHING"

and who was it that promised her if she got to a certain point
she would longer be?

and you have to wonder
when her body shatters the mirror
as she falls to the bathroom floor
and no one is around to hear-
does she make a sound?

and the heart rate

slows

        and slows.

            and

              slows

and

tell me about the day
you pulled my body from the lake-
how the water weighed me down
more than my thoughts
ever could
how I was so cold
you never thought
I'd find warmth again

but remember to tell me
I didn't drown,
that the sun rose the next day
and I rose with it

we don't know it yet,
but this love
was never meant for us

Dear Intimacy,

do you place your hopes in pennies?
or do you lock them away
in something more practical
(like Pandora's Box)
because let's be honest,
pennies are so easily misplaced,
and you don't want hope lost among the stars·
you want it somewhere secure; safe
where you know you can reach for it
when you need it

I place my pennies heads up
in the lobbies of skyscrapers.
sometimes I put hope in quarters
because pennies aren't quite big enough.
I'm not sure what to do with dollar bills though,
there seems to be too much of them
and not enough of me
do you dot your I's with stars?
or are you less focused on
becoming a constellation
and more on
becoming a better version of you?
I know sometimes we worry
we aren't good enough,
but I'll let you in on a little secret,

you are a star
on the verge of exploding
into something entirely
profound

do you loop your Y's around galaxies?
tracing the outline of every sun
every planet, every meteorite,
every wish carelessly tossed up there
ones that were not meant
for pennies and dandelions,
but saved special for shooting stars

are your O's really planets?
did you draw up our existence
into a tiny vowel?
you know,
if you were to draw yourself
just a little bigger
you could be the sun

I try to write in starlit stanzas,
because I like to think that
if I have stardust in my ink
I'll hold someone's heart in my words

my Y's coil around
all the dreams
I've lost along the way,
hoping to maybe find a few again

my O's are drawn extra large
maybe I just never want
to lose the sunlight

when you get cold, do you wrap yourself in downy dreams?
or do you prefer a blanket-
something softer and more solid
that you can feel in your hands
because you need blue cotton
the gentle, comforting touch of love

I wonder...
does it tickle your heart
when I lie with my head on your chest
breathing you in?

I (on the other hand)
need rays of hope and sunlit summers
because I find that last fleeting
happy thought you have
before falling asleep
is so much warmer
than anything woven from a careful hand.

when I lie with my head on your chest
I'm really counting your heartbeats
1...2...3...
and the breaths I would take
were I able to breathe
so (as usual) I am lost in the glow
of anticipation
and of a world that will never exist
except in my warm sleepy thoughts
please don't say "what if"-
for my heart is beginning to wonder
about the beautiful mess we could be

tonight, I am painting violets in the dark circles growing under my eyes as I curl under the covers, trying to quiet the panic rising in my chest

shhh
the rain has stopped

    (you can sleep now)

9:01 a.m.

today is one of those days where
I can't tell where I end
and you begin-
if you're touching me
or I'm touching you

       but it doesn't really matter
           (just don't leave yet)

-morning thoughts

I love you for how human you are

let us break and shatter and grow,
all while falling into one another

"it did not ruin her"
(so why is it ruining me?)

11:34 p.m.

I am curled
on the tile
under the stream
of scalding water

trying
to claw my way out
of this skin-

aching

for a body
that you
have never touched

I think I cut too deep.

the chaos is leaking out.

I am entirely too much void
and not enough stars

"I loved him more
than I've ever loved anything
and it almost killed me..."

3 a.m. conversations

I remembered again.
but in that moment I wasn't thinking about what had happened

I was just grateful for doors that lock and nights that end and hands that can't reach me anymore

crawl inside my hollow chest
and love me there.

where the light does not reach

they tell you how strong you are
how resilient

as if being called brave will suddenly make it easier to breathe
again

Number 24

trigger warning:
grey sheets
green flannels
rose scented perfume
and cinnamon candles

warning:
sometimes I don't know my own triggers

my lover's hand finds itself on the inside of my wrist
and the sunlit bedroom
turns to dark basements
and red cars
and blue couches
and her hands
start to
become his

warning:
sometimes the memories
leave me too shattered
to get through the day

need someone
to watch me today
make sure I eat today

lock the doors for me
today
and keep me away from
knives
and red cars
and men who look like
that incredibly tempting
first set of headlights
coming towards you
in oncoming traffic

trigger warning:
fireworks
crowded places
grey beanies
criminal minds
and loud spaces

he tells me no one
will ever love me the way he does
no one will be as perfect for me as he was

and he's right.

trigger warning:
no one will ever touch me the way he did
muffle my screams the way he did
speak to me the way he did

no one will ever again put a gun to my head
And pull the trigger

warning:
I will not let anyone
love me
the way he did

I don't know my own triggers
but I'm beginning to know my own worth

I tried so hard to tell you
that nothing would grow here
but you wouldn't listen

I showed you all the spaces
that the light could not reach
and told you everything
the water would not wash away,
but you came back
every day,
and refused to give up

I told you
over and over again
that I was not something
you could just walk in and try to fix
and you said,
"I'm not trying to fix you.
I am trying to help you blossom
into the brave person I know you are"

and I want to let you know,
that today, I am here-
surrounded by blossoming
new beginnings,

and if this finds you,
somewhere
somehow
thank you for never believing
that some people were not
meant to bloom

To E.M.L.-

do you remember when I called you from the hospital? You were one of the four phone numbers I wrote down, one of the four people I counted on to care.

I pulled at the scarlet stained bandages on my wrists and listened to the line ringing.

You answered. And when I told you what I had done, your voice took a tone that I didn't recognize.

You told me I was ruining all the hard work you put into my future, you reminded me that you were the one to build me up and you were the only reason I was still breathing. You told me I had wasted everything you had ever done for me. I cried and apologized, and the line went silent as you hung up.

And I shattered.

But that was a year ago. And today, I am here to tell you that you are not the reason I am standing here.

I am.

I am standing here, not because of you, but because of my bravery and my resiliency. You no longer get to take credit for everything I have become.

Because, I am not a product of your will and your care. You claim you built up my confidence, and you might have contributed, you gave me the first brick I needed, but I am the one who collected the next thousand. I am the one who took those bricks and built and rebuilt myself. I am the one who has gotten through every nightmare, every panic attack. I pulled myself out of the darkness. I am the one that chose recovery, and I am the one that continues to choose it, every fucking day.

You have never been the one behind my success and my recovery, it's always been me.

Thank you for the reminder,
Carmine Gothard

My sunshine,
My love, my life,
My reason for being,

Do you remember that perfect night we rested with our heads in the snow
Listening to Chasing Cars, trying to forget the world?
An infinity of stars dotted the sky, tugging at the darkness,
And hope was in our eyes, tugging at the ache of our empty hearts.

You were the sun, and as the moon
It was my job to ensure that you rose each morning,
But how to you make someone see the beauty of the flowers
When they don't even want to open their eyes?

When you would call to say that there was nothing left of you,
I would always answer on the first ring
Because I knew that if I took the chance of waiting until the third,
… You might not still be there…
You told me that we were made of paper
We were too fragile for hope and love
Because our paper hearts could only take so much
Before they would tear under the strain of all this
Aching and breaking and taking

I would spend hours writing you a tomorrow that you just might want to live,

In hopes that you would see the little beauty left in this world
I would write you warm rainy nights,
And white roses,
Coffee shop concerts,
And 11:11 wishes,
I painted you stars,
Ones that were not millions of light years away, on the verge of exploding,
But forever glittering in the infinite black canvas above our heads,
Ones that you could still wish on and place your hopes in when the darkness got to be too much.

My love,
My sunshine,

We might be only fragile paper girls in an unforgiving paper world
With torn paper hearts that have been taped back together, God knows how many times,
But we are closer to the stars than anyone ever will be
Because we know what it is to be set adrift into oblivion
We know what it is like to have to make your own light
Because we know what it is to live a life where there is none

Our stars are forged from the ashes of fallen wishes and built from the glittering bits of broken dreams and shattered skies
Our skies are hand painted with hints of gold, silver, blue, and hope mixed in with the blackness of it all
Our world may be made of just paper, but I will spend every waking moment covering it in poetry written across starlit stanzas and every color known to man
If it'll make you want to rise again each morning

we almost made it

& we were almost okay
& we were almost enough

& it was almost beautiful.

Victim to Survivor to Living-

"It's common with trauma victims…"

The phrase echoes through the classroom as I shift uncomfortably in my chair. It would be a few years before I figured out why I was so unsettled in that moment. But I know now.

The word victim is cruel. It is broken bodies left at crime scenes, perpetrators left somehow outside of the law. The word victim is "Ladies and Gentlemen of the jury, I present to you the victim's stolen sense of security and broken worth as evidence. I present to you this plastic bag of held breaths, shaky hands, and shattered dreams, and invite you to take a look at the bad touch that stains the body of my client." It is cruel. It echoes down crowded hallways and rests upon your forehead for everyone to see. It marks you as a Law and Order season finale, as someone deserving of pity filled eyes and the sympathetic hand on the shoulder, as a one in five, a "how much was she drinking?"

Even "survivor" has a strange connotation to it. I think it's supposed to sound brave. "I survived. I am stronger today because of what I have endured." but does it really count as surviving if you honest to god, sometimes find yourself wishing that they had killed you that night?

In the whole eleven years since IT happened, I have yet to find a word that fits right... I am not a survivor. Sometimes it feels like I am in between giving up and giving it my all. There are still nightmares and flashbacks and the pain of knowing that another human being has the potential and power to utterly destroy you... there is no remedy for memory. I am not surviving, I am just living.

BUT

I am not a victim. I am not a broken body broadcasted on the 11 o'clock news for your viewing pleasure. I am not some unfortunate tale for you, with all your unbroken pieces, to try and sympathize with. I am not a place to deposit your extra pity. I am not a one in five, I refuse to be a victim. I refuse to be some sad story mixed in with the rest. Because I might not be surviving, but I am sure as hell still living.

My Dear Friend,

When I heard what had happened to you, I cried in my closet for an hour... I cried a little for myself, and I know that's selfish... but most of my tears were for you. I wept for your favorite songs and for the colors you would fall out of love with, for the gentle hugs you would shrink away from, for the stars you would lose sight of... and all the things you wouldn't be able to forget.

And, my love, I am so terribly sorry that we can suddenly relate... I wish we could remain complete strangers with nothing in common, because I don't want you to have to share this label or story with me. Just know that this one terrible thing does not define you... even when you believe it does with every fiber of your being- you are so much more than this.

I can't promise you that next week you're going to wake up and feel okay again, but I can promise you that the dark days and long nights are temporary. "I know that in your condition the sunshine's been missing, but don't believe that it isn't there." Day by day, you'll get a little bit braver and a little bit stronger until you fall back in love with your favorite songs and colors, hugs will suddenly mean the world to you again, the night skies will be dotted with an infinity of stars, and the things you can't forget will become something you can someday make peace with.

You are not alone in your fight my love; I promise you this. I know that things can be dark and scary, but you're a shining star in this world full of darkness- your light will shine through. You didn't ask for this, nor did you do anything to deserve it. No matter what the circumstances were, this was not your fault. What happened was not fair, it wasn't right, it wasn't okay, it wasn't deserved... but most importantly, it's not who you are. What happened to you does not define you. "We are greater than the sum of our parts," (John Green) meaning, you are greater than your experiences. You are more than what happened to you, you are not one person's actions- you are what you choose to become. My love, you are made up of your favorite lyrics that you shout when you're driving alone, chasing the sunset. You are rainy nights spent under twinkly lights with the people who make you feel whole. You are your daughter's smile or your parents' joy. You're as infinite as the stars. You're fragile and strong, all at the same time. "It's a beautiful medley of constantly being broken down and pieced together. I am a painting almost done to completion, beautiful, but not quite complete." (Kate J.) You are brave, timeless, amazing, wonderful, welcomed, supported, courageous, innocent, talented, happy, hopeful, loved- you are all of these things and more.

Love always,
Carmine

www.ingramcontent.com/pod-product-compliance
Ingram Content Group UK Ltd.
Pitfield, Milton Keynes, MK11 3LW, UK
UKHW022241230426
12048UKWH00018BA/1390